EXTREME

War Machines

The Deadliest Weapons in History

M.J. Dougherty

A & C Black • London

Produced for A & C Black by

Monkey Puzzle Media Ltd
Little Manor Farm, Brundish,
Woodbridge, Suffolk IP13 8BL, UK

Published by A & C Black Publishers Limited
36 Soho Square, London W1D 3QY

First published 2009

ISBN 978-1-4081-1476-6 (hardback)
ISBN 978-1-4081-1996-9 (paperback)

A CIP catalogue record for this book is available
from the British Library.

Editor: Susie Brooks
Design: Mayer Media Ltd
Picture research: Lynda Lines
Series consultants: Jane Turner and James de Winter

This book is produced using paper that is made
from wood grown in managed, sustainable forests.
It is natural, renewable and recyclable. The logging
and manufacturing processes conform to the
environmental regulations of the country of origin.

Printed in Singapore by Tien Wah Press

Picture acknowledgements
akg-images 21 top right (ullstein bild), 26 (ullstein
bild); Alamy pp. 6 (North Wind Picture Archives),
7 (North Wind Picture Archives), 12 (Paris Pierce);
Art Archive pp. 10 (Musée du Château de Versailles/
Gianni Dagli Orti), 13 (Musée Carnavelet, Paris/
Gianni Dagli Orti); Corbis pp. 14 (Skyscan), 16
bottom right; Getty Images pp. 22 top left, 24 (AFP),
27; iStockphoto p. 11; MPM Images pp. 9, 22–23;
Photolibrary.com pp. 8 (The British Library), 15
(Age Fotostock/Chris Mattison); Reuters pp. 1
(Rick Wilking), 18 centre right (Oleg Popov), 18–19
(Rick Wilking), 20–21 (Kamal Kishore), 25 (Hamad
Mohammed); Rex Features p. 5 (John Mills);
Topfoto.co.uk pp. 28 (Lightroom/US Navy);
Wikimedia Commons pp. 4 (US Federal
Government, 16–17 US Marine Corps, 29 (US
Federal Government).

The front cover shows an SR-71 Blackbird
reconnaissance plane (MPM Images/Digital Vision).

CONTENTS

Abbreviations km stands for kilometres • **mm** stands for millimetres • **in** stands for inches • **km/h** stands for kilometres per hour • **mph** stands for miles per hour

Aim... fire, fire, fire!

You've got 30 bullets in your assault rifle. Within three seconds you could have shot them all, at a target half a kilometre away.

Most soldiers use assault rifles. They are light, tough and can fire a stream of bullets. This is called "automatic fire". Some assault rifles also have a **grenade** launcher built in.

*This rifle has an advanced **sight**. The big tube underneath is a grenade launcher.*

The very best soldiers are trained to use **sniper** rifles. To be a sniper, it's not enough to be a good shot. You also have to be good at sneaking around and hiding from the enemy. A good sniper is almost invisible.

grenade a small bomb   **sight** the eyepiece on a rifle that helps the gunman to aim

These soldiers are using a powerful Barrett sniper rifle. Its bullet can travel almost 7 km (4.3 miles).

SPOTTER: uses **binoculars** to find more targets

TELESCOPIC SIGHT: lets the sniper see the target

BIPOD: supports the weight of the rifle

Blast!

Snipers can shoot radios, machine guns and other important equipment to stop the enemy from using it.

sniper a gunman who shoots from a hidden place   **binoculars** a device for viewing distant objects

Capturing a castle

You need to get into that castle. Simple – build a machine to help you climb over the walls. Or you could just smash them down with a battering ram!

Using a ladder to climb up castle walls was extremely dangerous! It was a bit safer to build a siege tower. Siege towers were like staircases on wheels, which could be pushed up to the castle walls. The strong sides of the tower protected the soldiers as they climbed up.

Another way to get into a castle was to smash a hole in the wall with a battering ram. This was a big, heavy beam that could knock down a wall or castle gate, if it hit hard enough.

Soldiers climb up inside the siege tower and then run across a bridge onto the castle walls.

force a push or a pull

Tip of ram concentrates **force** over a small area.

Heavy ram moving fast has lots of energy.

Concentrated force = lots of **pressure**.

Heave!

FORCE

Pressure pushes stones out of the wall.

Fire!

Soldiers inside a castle tried to set fire to enemy war machines by firing burning arrows at them.

One of these battering rams is supported by a special frame. The other one is just held up by strong men!

pressure a measure of the amount of force acting on something

Slinging stones

**Problem: You're guarding a castle when you see a giant rock-slinging machine outside.
Solution: Get out of the way – fast!**

A trebuchet was a powerful machine that hurled large stones. It took a long time to build one, but once it was ready it could smash any castle wall. Many castles surrendered once the defenders saw a trebuchet outside.

Trebuchets were no use against a moving target. Enemy soldiers could just run out of the way of the rock. They were also very difficult to aim and move around. So they were not used in battles, just against castles.

This very old picture shows soldiers attacking a castle with a trebuchet.

gravity a force that attracts objects to each other

4 Rock goes this way!

These trebuchets were built recently by people who were investigating how trebuchets worked.

1 Put a really big rock in here.

Flinging things

A trebuchet could release up to 2,000 stones in one day. Other weapons thrown from trebuchets included darts, fireballs, dung and even dead body parts!

2 **Gravity** pulls this box full of heavy weights down.

3 Arm swings up on **pivot**.

GRAVITY

pivot a device around which a lever can turn or swing

Shooting arrows

The enemy is way over there. You're over here. So how do you fight them? It's not a problem if you've got archers armed with bows and arrows.

In the Middle Ages, English soldiers used powerful longbows that could punch their arrows right through a knight's metal **armour**. They could shoot many arrows at an enemy before he got close enough to use his sword.

The solid part of a bow is called the bowstave. It is made of **flexible** material that bends when you pull back on the string. This stores energy. When you are ready to shoot the arrow, you just let go of the string. The stored energy is released, sending the arrow speeding on its way.

These archers are aiming along their arrows, straight at their targets. If they wanted to shoot further they would aim upwards.

archer someone who shoots with a bow and arrows

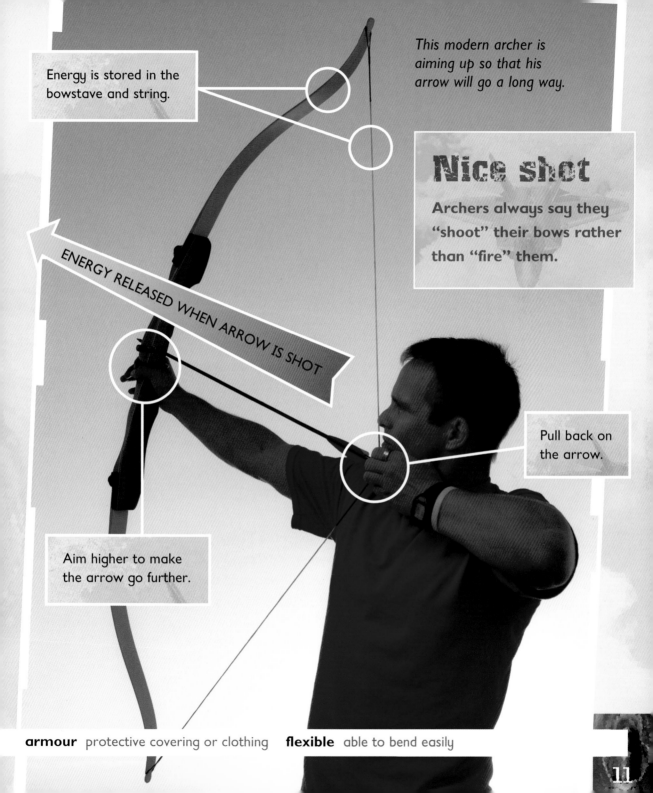

Energy is stored in the bowstave and string.

This modern archer is aiming up so that his arrow will go a long way.

ENERGY RELEASED WHEN ARROW IS SHOT

Nice shot

Archers always say they "shoot" their bows rather than "fire" them.

Pull back on the arrow.

Aim higher to make the arrow go further.

armour protective covering or clothing   **flexible** able to bend easily

11

Big guns

Load in some gunpowder and a cannonball. Point your cannon at the enemy. Light the fuse and stand back. BOOM! Bye bye enemy.

Wooden ships could easily be sunk by cannon fire – so armoured warships like this one were invented.

Once cannons were invented, there was no point in hiding in a castle. People who had cannons could just blast you to pieces! Sailors started putting cannons on their ships, too, so that they could win sea battles.

A cannon uses gunpowder to fire its cannonball. The cannon has to be made from very strong materials like brass or iron. If it is too weak, it explodes when you fire it.

gunpowder a mixture of chemicals that burns very quickly

These cannons are being fired high into the air so that their cannonballs drop on the enemy.

1 Energy is stored in gunpowder.

BOOM!

4 Energy sends the cannonball this way.

2 Light the fuse and step back...

3 Gunpowder explodes, releasing energy.

Battery power

A group of cannons is called a "battery", because they were originally used to batter down castle walls.

fuse a cord that carries a flame to start an explosion

Knights of the skies

The pilot sits right behind his guns.
He aims by pointing the whole plane!

Your enemies keep sending planes over to drop bombs on you and to spy on what you're up to. So what do you do? You send fighter planes to shoot them down!

At first pilots shot at each other with pistols, or even threw bricks. This didn't work very well. Soon special planes with machine guns were invented. The pilot had to point his plane straight at the enemy to fire. Today's fighter planes are a lot more advanced!

Fighting flops

The first fighter planes sometimes fell apart on their own, without even being shot at!

A fighter plane has to move quickly to stay in the sky. Air moving fast over the wings creates **lift** – and if there's not enough lift, gravity pulls the plane down. A big, heavy plane needs to go faster or have bigger wings – or both!

lift a combination of forces that keeps a plane in the air

This is one of the best early fighter planes, used by the famous German pilot known as the Red Baron.

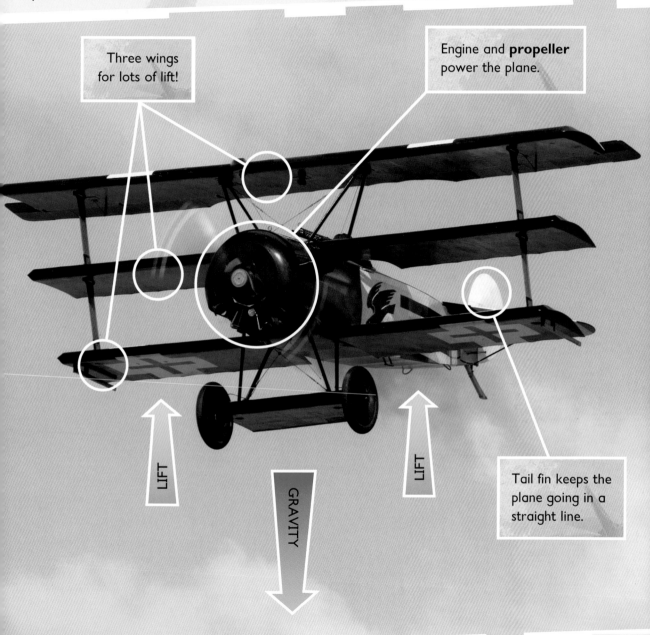

Three wings for lots of lift!

Engine and **propeller** power the plane.

LIFT

GRAVITY

LIFT

Tail fin keeps the plane going in a straight line.

propeller a set of blades that rotates to push against air or water

Tank tactics

You've got a big gun to fight with, you can climb over just about anything, and bullets just bounce off you. That's what it's like to be in a tank!

Tanks were invented to attack enemy machine guns. They had to be able to cross wide **trenches** and muddy ground to get near the enemy. Modern tanks are much faster and better protected than the originals, but they do a similar job.

Tanks are protected by plates of armour, made from strong materials like steel, and by being able to move fast. This makes them hard to hit. Tanks need powerful engines, because all that armour is very heavy!

The first tanks had tracks all the way round so that they could climb over obstacles.

trench a long ditch dug by soldiers to hide from the enemy

16

Leaping machine

During World War II, British inventors once fitted a tank with rockets so it could jump over obstacles!

A powerful engine drives the tank at up to 72 km/h (45 mph).

Gun has a **range** of up to 4 km (2.5 miles).

Tracks help the tank to cross rough ground.

Heavy armour protects the crew inside.

range the distance a bullet or missile will travel

Firepower

If you want serious firepower, you need a machine gun that can fire up to a thousand bullets every minute! It keeps on firing until you let go of the trigger.

This tank commander has a heavy machine gun to defend his tank if he needs to.

When a gun is fired, a small explosion goes off inside. This explosion pushes out in all directions, making the bullet go one way and the gun the other. Because the bullet is small and light, it travels much further and faster than the heavy gun.

The "kicking back" of a gun is called **recoil**. It can cause the weapon to jump around, making it hard to aim. Soldiers are taught to fire machine guns in short bursts, so that they waste fewer bullets.

trigger the lever used to fire a gun

The US army has used this type of M60 machine gun for 50 years.

Fast fire

The M249 machine gun can fire more than 15 bullets a second!

POW!

Gun kicks back this way.

Bullet goes this way – fast!

Bullet fires from in here.

Hot gas comes out with the bullet.

recoil the backward jerk from a gun when it is fired

The biggest guns of all

Enemy soldiers are 80 kilometres (50 miles) away. They think they're safe – but they're not! Artillery weapons can attack targets so far away that the people firing the weapons don't even see the shots land.

The big guns and rocket launchers of the artillery fire high into the air. Eventually, gravity brings the **shell** or rocket back down to fall on the enemy. The part that harms the enemy is called a warhead. Many warheads contain chemicals that store a lot of energy and release it as a big explosion. These are called high-explosive warheads.

Some artillery weapons are towed behind trucks. Others are built into a vehicle so that they can be driven around. When artillery weapons fire and then move, this is called "Shoot and Scoot".

These rocket launchers are mounted on trucks so that they can move around.

High-explosive warhead

Super shell

The biggest gun of all time fired a shell 80 centimetres (31.5 inches) across, which weighed nearly 5 tons.

artillery big weapons that fire at far-off targets

That shell will come down a long way away! The gun is an M198 **howitzer**, with a range of up to 22.5 km (14 miles).

Rocket flies this way.

Burning chemicals release energy.

Crew launch the rockets from the truck cab.

Energy pushes the rocket forward.

shell a container of explosives, fired from a gun   **howitzer** an artillery gun with a short barrel

Sneaky submarines

Your job is to sneak up on enemy ships, sink them and then escape without being spotted. That's easy if you're in a submarine.

*This submarine is well **streamlined** to help it go fast underwater.*

The first submarines had guns as well as **torpedoes**. They often stayed on the surface to attack their enemies. This was very dangerous! Enemy ships could shoot back, or even ram the submarine like a dodgem and sink it.

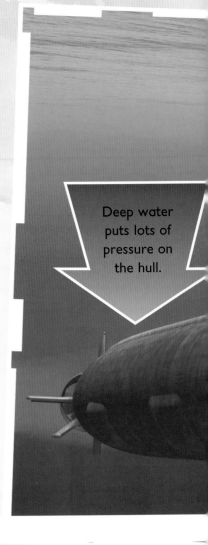

Deep water puts lots of pressure on the hull.

streamlined shaped so that air or water flows easily over it

Boom!

Submarines that can launch nuclear missiles are called Boomers.

Modern submarines do not have guns. They attack with torpedoes and sometimes **missiles** launched from underwater. Some submarines can stay underwater for months at a time. They carry a lot of torpedoes so that they can sink several ships.

A torpedo is a bit like a tiny, fast submarine packed with explosives.

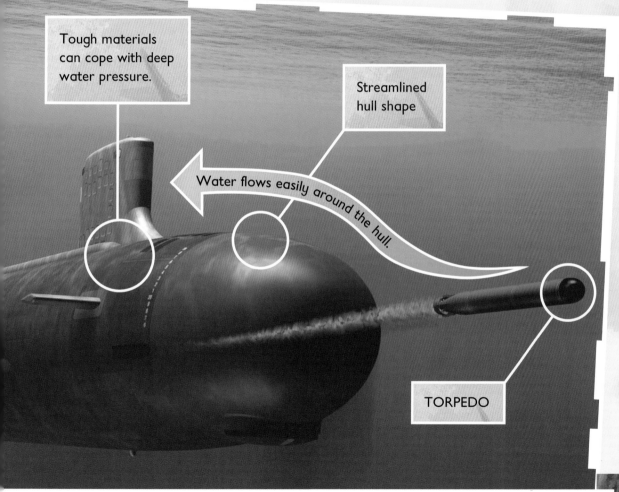

Tough materials can cope with deep water pressure.

Streamlined hull shape

Water flows easily around the hull.

TORPEDO

torpedo an underwater weapon   **missile** a rocket that can be guided to the target

Floating airfields

Aircraft carriers are like floating airfields. They can go anywhere in the world. A carrier uses different types of aircraft, including fighters, strike planes and helicopters. Each has a different job to do.

Planes take off from the front of the aircraft carrier. They are usually launched using a **catapult**, to help them get enough speed to fly. It is possible to launch planes while others are landing.

A US Navy aircraft carrier can have 60–90 aircraft on board.

Nickname

Aircraft carriers are sometimes called Flat-Tops, because of their shape.

strike planes planes that attack targets on the ground

Planes land on the landing deck at the rear of the ship. To help them stop quickly, planes have a hook that catches wires on the landing deck. Without this, planes would go straight off the end into the sea!

A US Navy Hornet aircraft lands on a carrier.

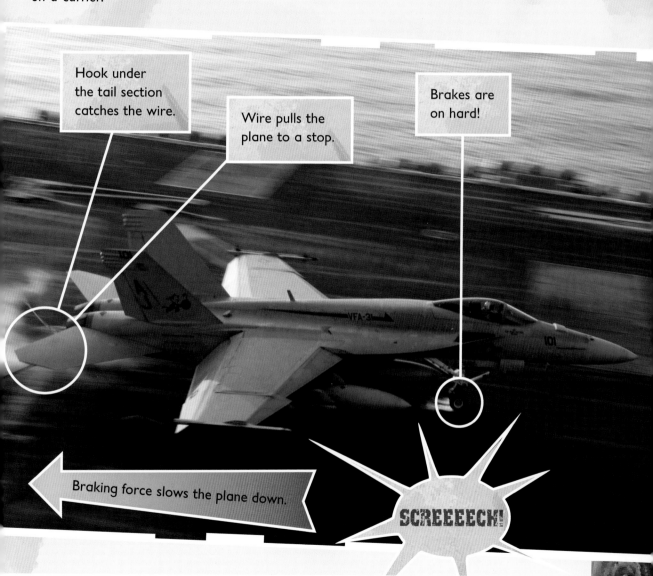

Hook under the tail section catches the wire.

Wire pulls the plane to a stop.

Brakes are on hard!

Braking force slows the plane down.

SCREEEECH!

catapult a launching device used to propel planes or missiles into take-off

Flying attacks

You can fly faster than the speed of sound. You've got missiles and guns to shoot down other planes. You're almost unbeatable. That's what it's like to be a fighter pilot!

Modern **combat** aircraft fight each other using missiles and guns. They can also attack ships or targets on the ground using rockets, missiles and bombs. Planes can fly to targets that soldiers on the ground could not get to. BANG! They do their work and then get back to base in just a few hours.

Bombers and attack aircraft are designed to destroy targets on the ground. Fighters shoot down other planes. Some aircraft can do more than one job. They are called multirole aircraft.

Missiles are used to shoot down other planes from a distance.

Supersonic

The SR-71 Blackbird can fly at over three times the speed of sound.

combat fighting

The F-22 Raptor is one of the best combat aircraft ever built.

Two powerful engines for high speed

Strong but light materials

Streamlined shape

Smart weapons

You need to destroy something that's hard to hit. Easy – use a smart weapon! These amazing missiles can be guided straight at a tricky target.

This Javelin missile can detect the heat from an aircraft engine.

Some smart weapons are guided using a joystick, a lot like flying a small plane. Some are guided with a **laser beam**. They look for the spot the laser is lighting up and fly to it. This means that you can change target while the weapon is in flight if you want to destroy something different, or if the target moves.

Some really smart weapons can find the target all by themselves! They may use **radar** or detect heat. Some have a **GPS** system (like a Sat Nav in a car) to show them where to go.

laser beam a narrow strip of very bright light   **radar** using radio waves to locate something

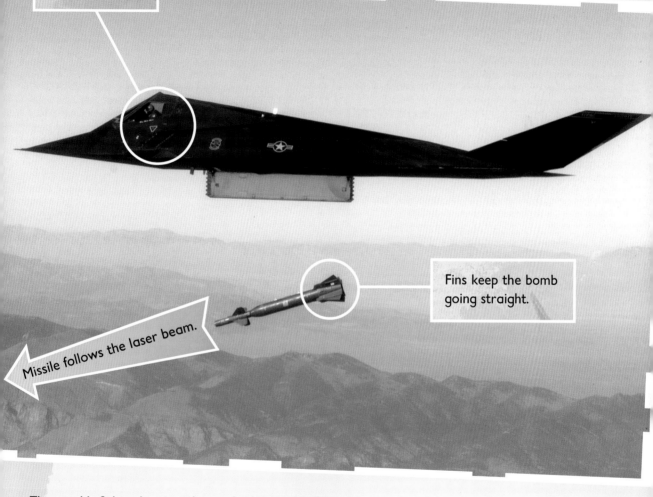

Hole in two

Using smart weapons, it is possible to blow a hole in a wall with one missile, then fly the next one through it!

Fighter shines a laser beam on the target.

Fins keep the bomb going straight.

Missile follows the laser beam.

This stealth fighter has just dropped a laser-guided bomb.

GPS a system for finding a location using space satellites

Glossary

archer someone who shoots with a bow and arrows

armour protective covering or clothing

artillery big weapons that fire at far-off targets

binoculars a device for viewing distant objects

catapult a launching device used to propel planes or missiles into take-off

combat fighting

flexible able to bend easily

force a push or a pull

fuse a cord that carries a flame to start an explosion

GPS a system for finding a location using space satellites

gravity a force that attracts objects to each other

grenade a small bomb

gunpowder a mixture of chemicals that burns very quickly

howitzer an artillery gun with a short barrel

laser beam a narrow strip of very bright light

lift a combination of forces that keeps a plane in the air

missile a rocket that can be guided to the target

pivot a device around which a lever can turn or swing

pressure a measure of the amount of force acting on something

propeller a set of blades that rotates to push against air or water

radar using radio waves to locate something

range the distance a bullet or missile will travel

recoil the backward jerk from a gun when it is fired

shell a container of explosives, fired from a gun

sight the eyepiece on a rifle that helps the gunman to aim

sniper a gunman who shoots from a hidden place

streamlined shaped so that air or water flows easily over it

strike planes planes that attack targets on the ground

torpedo an underwater weapon used in attacking ships

trench a long ditch dug by soldiers to hide from the enemy

trigger the lever used to fire a gun

Further information

Books

Amazing Ships: Aircraft Carriers by John Sutherland, Diane Canwell (Gareth Stevens Publishing, 2007)
A simple introduction to what aircraft carriers do and how they do it.

Amazing Ships: Submarines by John Sutherland and Diane Canwell (Gareth Stevens Publishing, 2007)
A simple introduction to what submarines do and how they do it.

Small Arms: From the Civil War to the Present Day by Martin J. Dougherty (Amber Books, 2008)
A history of rifles, pistols, shotguns and machine guns.

Tanks: Compared and Contrasted by Martin J. Dougherty (Barnes & Noble, 2005)
A history of tanks, including "head to head" comparisons of famous designs.

Battles That Changed Warfare by Devries, Dougherty, Jorgensen, Mann and McNab (Amber Books, 2008)
Deals with battles where a new weapon (war machine) had a decisive impact.

Extreme: How to Catapult a Castle by James de Winter (A & C Black, 2008)
Packed full of information on how to attack a castle – with battering rams, giant catapults and flaming arrows – and how to defend it.

Websites

www.probertencyclopaedia.com/war.htm
Comprehensive reference on weapons and warfare.

www.middle-ages.org.uk/siege-weapons.htm
Detailed information on knights, castles, weapons and siege equipment of the Middle Ages.

www.geocities.com/Athens/Academy/7967/web2.htm
Information on castles and sieges.

www.battletanks.com/
Information and pictures of important tank designs from many countries.

Films

The Lighthorsemen directed by Simon Wincer (AFC, 1987)
Based on the true story of a band of Australian cavalrymen, fighting in Turkey during World War I. Follow them as they bravely charge on horseback towards the enemy.

Top Gun directed by Tony Scott (Konami, 1986)
A US Navy fighter pilot goes to the "Top Gun" fighter school to train with the best pilots around. He then returns to his aircraft carrier in time to take part in a massive air battle.

Index